Jonestown:
A Vexation

JONESTOWN: A VEXATION

Poems by

Carmen Gillespie

Detroit
Lotus Press

Lotus Press, Inc.
"Flower of a New Nile"
Post Office Box 21607
Detroit, Michigan 48221
www.lotuspress.org

Foreword

This book was born in the skies over Guyana in the 1970s when I was about twelve years old. My father was working for the government of Guyana as a helicopter pilot to the then prime minister, Forbes Burnham. Because of my father's work, we were able to fly often into the dense, lush interior of Guyana, an experience that catalyzed a primal feeling of connection and curiosity about this most unusual and fraught land. My family and I left Guyana in the spring of 1978, months before the mass deaths of members of the Peoples Temple at Jonestown.

According to the historical record, the spelling of Peoples Temple omits the apostrophe. All direct quotations from Jim Jones and Peoples Temple members come from the Jonestown tapes. Occasional grammatical errors in the quoted material have been retained. The tapes were discovered at the site of the Jonestown massacre and were transcribed by affiliates of the Jonestown Institute, http://jonestown.sdsu.edu. I would like to acknowledge the important work of the archive as a repository of the story of Jonestown and the Peoples Temple. I particularly acknowledge Fielding McGehee for his work creating and maintaining the institute and for his assistance obtaining a cover photo for the book.

Thank you to Shara McCallum for your support and friendship during the creation of this book. Your editorial suggestions and advice were crucial. Meenakshi Ponnuswami, thank you for support and unwavering confidence in this project and for your loving presence. I am grateful also to my friends and colleagues, Harriet Pollack and Linden Lewis. Thanks to Constance Timm for the cover design. I am indebted to the Cave Canem family and to its founders, Toi Derricotte and Cornelius Eady. Rane Arroyo, thank you for taking me seriously as a poet and Joanne Gabbin for including me always, but especially in the Wintergreen Collective.

I would be deeply remiss if I did not thank Naomi Long Madgett for her work supporting African American poetry and for the contest that enabled this book to be published.

This book would not have happened without the unwavering support of my husband, Harold Bakst, who listened to my ideas, helped me process all of the complications and agonies of this story, and read and reread every draft with artful and meticulous scrutiny. As always, thank you, Chelsea and Delaney. You smell like sunshine.

This book is dedicated to Guyana
and to the lost souls of Jonestown.

Contents

vex·a·tion

\vek-sā-shən\ Origin: 1400s; Latin. From *vexationem* (vexatio). Contemporarily losing usage except in areas of the English-speaking Caribbean. Particularly common and nuanced in Guyanese vernacular.

—noun

1.   A self-destructive experience or occurrence whose significance, although profound, becomes indistinct with the passage of time.

2.   The feeling created when the root cause of a situation is elusive, indeterminate, or misunderstood.

3.   A reoccurring perception, much like déjà vu, created when two disparate entities bear disquieting and instructive commonalities.

4.   An entity, situation, memory, or place that eludes definition or fixedness.

5.   A long-standing injustice, the injury of which is suffered as a direct result of another's duplicity.

6.   A profound, yet unfulfilled, desire or need.

1.   A self-destructive experience or occurrence whose significance, although profound, becomes indistinct with the passage of time.

Guyana is the only English-speaking country in South America. Contemporarily, Guyana has the highest suicide rate of any country in the Western Hemisphere. Guyana's original inhabitants were Amerindians, most prominently the Arawaks and the Caribs. The Europeans first arrived in Guyana in the late 1400s. In part, their motivation to conquer and colonize Guyana came from the story of El Dorado, a mythical land with gold so abundant that men and women rolled in it, covering their skin like powder. The Europeans forced the Amerindians to work for them as slaves. Later, the European settlers would enslave kidnapped Africans as a labor force. In 1763, there was a major slave revolt in the Guyanese town of Berbice. Led by Cuffy (or Kofi), a house slave trained as a cooper, the revolt was unsuccessful. After his defeat, Cuffy killed several of his accomplices and then took his own life. In the 1870s, an Amerindian named Awacuipu led nearly 400 fellow Amerindians to kill each other and themselves in a mystical attempt to acquire white skin and, they believed, freedom and equality. The Soucoyant is a mythical figure in Guyanese and Caribbean cultures who is said to travel nightly in a ball of fire in a quest for blood. She can be prevented by salt. On November 18, 1978, more than 900 residents of Jonestown, Guyana died in a mass murder/suicide massacre. In the years following the massacre, the Jonestown site has been burned at least three times. The residents of Jonestown were members of an American religious/ideological organization they called The Peoples Temple. Many members believed that they came to Jonestown to pioneer a new inclusive way of life. The Peoples Temple was founded and run by a man named Jim Jones.

There:

distant ocean
sieves noon-time
equatorial sun
into nearly
a thousand

refractions
falling bright as blame
and, for a moment, the air
glints electric—
thick and ungrounded—
and invisibly seeds
a yawning hot

harvest
sweltering beneath
crackling hush—
the bush dripping
mossy and unmolested

Deluge of Days

adrift in green grown to the eye
phantom doorframes float in grasses
resistant to memory
and machete—
jungletown drowned in the deluge of days
like a wooden ship in the times
before news was synaptic

times when the final report
of five headed west in a wagon
was written in orange yarn—
      homemade hair from the baby's doll—
embroidered on spent
embrittled twigs

Equatorial November

It's that time of year when,
from far coasts, winds dance
and disagree,
tango becoming violent
vortex of unrestrained
advance, approach
illicit, predatory,
and loud—
clanging bells clapper
prayers in petition
to what may
come.

Inventory:

1) metal remains
    rusting, shadowing the soil like spill
    boiled over from unstirred pots

2) fruiting trees—
    rooted by hands grown now unfleshed—
        stand puzzling the endless season
        of alien sun
            and still bear forth on bony
            leafless limbs

3) hunger

Hunger

Its reach is the yearn of Adam
toward His hand
or of earth-clotted shoots
toward sun
or of the young, opened mouth,
expectant and assured, arched
toward the spoon
and its source.

The Soucoyant

What is left
for me to suck?
Nothing but the space
where teeth used to set.

Having flown far through this land,
so scarce of human hand
and feet, I scented afar
a feast. But I came
too late for the blood-
letting and am disgusted
with these amateur
and salty souls, who dream
only of a way back home
across the waters.

El Dorado

Each time a story—
gold, or land, or freedom—
rebirth in a place
where no one knows your name
    or status
        as second son
        with a barren hold

    or dance
        on the toes of the law,
        that final shuffled slip
        a die cast
            out and out and out.

Elusive Guyana,
Paradise,
where even other men
can be owned,
enslaved to a tale
by the shackles of hope
and the whip of possibility.

Sorrow Song of El Dorado:
by Sir Walter Raleigh, 1595*
(with coda to be repeated every hundred years)

I.
The fruit thereof
was long before fallen from the tree,
and the dead stock only remained.
I did therefore, even in the winter of my life,
undertake these travails, fitter for bodies
less blasted—
for men of greater ability.

I had knowledge, by relation, of that mighty,
rich, and beautiful empire of Guiana,
and of that great and golden city,
which the Spaniards call El Dorado.

I wandered 400 miles by land and river;
the country hath more quantity of gold—
the best parts of the Indies—slaves,
woods, rivers, and mines. If I should name
them, it would seem incredible to the reader.

Because there came ill with the good,
I hope the better sort will judge me
by themselves. The way of deceit
is not the way of honour or good opinion.

*Text found and extracted from *The Discovery of Guiana*, written by Sir
Walter Raleigh, 1595.

My intelligence was far from truth,
further from the sea
than was I.

II.
In time, without hope of life,
certain servants of the emperor,
having prepared gold made into fine powder,
blow it through hollow canes upon their naked bodies,
until they be all shining from the foot to the head;
and in this sort they sit drinking by twenties and hundreds,
and continue in drunkenness together.

Such a one rebelled,
putting to death so many as refused to be his followers,
and, finding no way to escape, he first put to the sword
his own children, foretelling them that they should not live
to be defamed or upbraided after his death.
He would yet deliver them from shame and reproach.

These were the ends and tragedies—
night strong poison
betrayed on all sides.

III.
Guiana,
it was the end of my journey.
The breeze and easterly wind
bloweth directly into the same,
that labyrinth of rivers,

either out or in, past ebbing and flowing—
only the thick and troubled water
digested and purged.

Mortality endureth the most insufferable torment
and abideth a most ugly and lamentable
death,
sometimes dying stark mad,
       and so unsavory as no man can endure.

The loss cried out
with so main a cry that all the woods echoed
between islands and broken ground
of that which nature, without labour,
bringeth forth.

Deck his skull with feathers of all colours,
and hang allgold plates about the bones
of this arms, thighs, and legs,
to spell one the other at the hour's end—
broken and tired,
ready to give up the ghost by the water's side
as if used to a keeper's call
and nearness of the land.

IV.
It is time to leave Guiana to the sun,
worthy of her grace—
so much heat, such outrageous
and contrary winds.

14

The Berbice Slave Revolt—1763: The Cooper

Making barrels took time
each stave bowed
with feet planted,
cosseted planks like arms
diving towards the sea
and bending in strength,
bending in strength.

The curve of their machetes
raised in unison
like the ribs of Leviathan,
pushed the whites north.
For a time, light seeped
through the opened
spaces

But there was no metal
to hoop allegiance,
to alter the warp
of words like house
and field.

Gathering close,
his men bowed 'round.
Cuffy knighted them
with a blow of his adze,
sharp against each temple.

And, he did not remove from his hands
their spent blood
before cursing the plantationed lands
with his own.

Awacaipu

When he returned home from the whites,
he brought his people
The Truth
written on paper they could not read
in a language that was rain
on the sea.

He carefully unfolded the smeary,
newsprinted sheets from the coast,
told them to hasten their advance
toward the way of all flesh,
to find in death
remedy for the deaf ears of their gods—
ill-equipped for liquid prayer words
like genocide, slavery, treaty, epidemic,
extinction.

Awacaipu called them up the mountain
to trade their souls for new skins, white
as light raying fingers through night trees.

Like Kabli moths, they came, lured
by the moon and its glowing
and faceless assurance.

2. The feeling created when the root cause of a situation is elusive, indeterminate, or misunderstood.

Jim Jones was born and raised in Indiana to parents James Thurmond Jones and Lynetta Putnam Jones. Jones's father was purported to be a Ku Klux Klan member. By all accounts, his parents were neglectful and distant, yet Jones developed a fervent adoration of his mother. Former friends reported that, even as a child, he exhibited peculiar and controlling behaviors. While in high school, Jim Jones led a pep rally that consisted of his preaching a mock funeral for the opposing team. At one point, Jones sold pet monkeys door to door to earn money. Jim Jones cobbled together various theologies and political philosophies to create an original and self-serving ideological base for the institution he created, The Peoples Temple. Services at the Temple were a study in spectacle and often included healings by Jones. A key component of his organization was the appearance of complete racial integration, an inclusiveness that was unheard of in 1950s Indiana. Feeling threatened by the status quo and by his increasing paranoia about the danger of nuclear annihilation, he moved his flock to Ukiah in Northern California. In California, The Peoples Temple grew, eventually establishing headquarters in San Francisco and Los Angeles. Jim Jones became an influential figure in Northern California and was lauded by many public officials, including Willie Brown, Angela Davis, Rosalynn Carter, Harvey Milk, George Moscone, and others. He became a legal and illegal drug abuser. He also engaged in sexual acts with many Temple members, both male and female. He told his followers that he engaged in sexual acts only for the benefit of the involved parishioner and that having sex with him would help to heal and purify his congregants. When former members began complaining about abuse and violence in the organization and newspapers began to investigate the claims, Jones began the process of relocating the membership to Guyana.

Little Child

From the beginning,
the black mark at the center
of the kitten's paw
spiraled 'round
and mapped its end.
Jimmy saw the sign,
watched its darkness spread
through the soul
of the mewling creature.

Oh, he loved it. Cared for it,
shielding its soft bones from boots
and empty bottles
thrown without passion
by his parents
from the porch.

But salvation was different.
He knew redemption
required sacrifice.

In the end he was fast
and used a blade so sharp
the kitten's mouth and eyes
remained open
in eternal surprise.

Box in hand,
he gathered them,
the six or seven girls and boys,
    suffer the little children . . .
made them hold hands
as his words fell
like the distinct plash
    of drops from an Indiana
summer storm,
pooling meaningless
in their corn stalk eyes.

Lightning Strikes

The stormy ripening of boy
into man split him—
softwood rent to its roots.

Fulmination flashing
like visible darkness,
left one half straight,

while the other arced skyward
then down, whittled
into blackened heart half.

Surfing Integration

"You're not integrated, and that's why you're having trouble in your mind." — Jim Jones

First white man in Indiana
legally to call a black boy
son, fighting for an end
to separation and segre-
gation, he made a family
small and large out of
difference, understanding
the tender places on black
flesh where bruises marked
dark skin and the worry
lines etching young white
faces with guilt
       that answered to names:
       Emmett, Malcolm, Medgar,
          Martin.

Wading through the bloody current, finger
to the wind, he knew he could ride the tide
and appear, as if by magic,
to walk on water.

Found Poem: Building the Peoples Temple

"Some
of you here,
you think you're white
and you got that, that inner soul spirit
and you feel that vibration for freedom and
you got that love for oh, justice and   and then there is
something to this, an intrinsic appreciation for art, aesthetics,
and rhythm, and you feel it in you and you look white, but
honey,
a nigger slipped in your woodpile somewhere."

— Jim Jones

Slaying Dragons: 1965-1976

Heaving from pent-up
pressures,
the land buckled and spaces,
after long labors,
opened.

Surveying the terrain
with an astigmatic gaze,
he mistook hunger for adoration,
but read their pock marks, like Braille.
With fingers' ease he drew
       the dreamers, the
       discriminated, the
       downtrodden, the
       dismissed, the drug-
addicted to his side, then sent them
jousting towards his imagined dragons,
forever rumbling just beyond.

The Minister's Black Veil

"His converts always regarded him with a dread peculiar to themselves ..." —Nathaniel Hawthorne

He perched behind mirrored frames,
always ready to reach through
thin skin for tumors, imagined
and real—
a sadistic sinner shrouded in shades,
finding sanctuary in the tint of shadows.

He dared them to stare
and witness,
the wickedness tunneling
their hearts—
sin, he said, like maggots
roving
through rotten flesh.

Master of Ceremonies

After a while
it didn't matter
what he said:

> Feed the hungry
> Clothe the naked
> Join together
> Stop racism
> Heal the sick

They believed.
He deceived with sleight of hand.
Chicken livers became tumors removed.

These miracles,
common as air,
sustained the spin
of the whirling plate.
Watching it aloft,
they believed he
would keep it up
and twirling
forever.

The Road to Gilead

"quoth the raven. . . "   — Edgar Allan Poe

Falling, he hissed to needle,
spoon, or pill, "Tell me truly,
I implore."

Then thought he heard
the Jordan whisper,
"It is there, on the other
shore."

Haiku for the White Knight

His knighthood was a
sword heavy and lowering
towards their outstretched necks.

"I wish I had learned more, such a healthy feeling of knowing how to do things with your hand, even though I'm a— I have a college degree, I feel like I never ah, never really knew how to do anything of a practical nature. No—Nonetheless, we continue on. We continue on, Peoples Temple, found the solution, agricultural project, found the solution in its legal services, a drug rehabilitation program, physical therapy, in its medical facilities. All this ballyhoo about healing — and I certainly can heal, and would be glad to take polytaph, polygra . . . "

Lead us not . . .

Such sacrifice was trying—
depleting to the body
of him
whose flesh claimed
no pleasure while purifying
the sinners
            with his sin.

Our father bestowing grace,
hal-lo-wed forgiveness laced
with liquor store communion
wine.

Our kingdom come.
Thy will be done.
On earth as it is
in . . .
Consuming, at most,
crumbs from this host.

Our Father, who
art . . . forever
and ever,

Amen.

Loaves of Fish

they were fed—
the hollow multitudes

too hungry, perhaps,
to notice
the loaves ashen
and the fishes rancid,
having too long departed
the sea

Exodus

The walls of water
began to collapse,
suspended miracle
giving way.

No Moses,
he ran them west,
then south,
losing orientation in the surge
               and the ferment
                    and the churn.

Jonesing: 1974

riding through the bush
on the only road
there
he saw green as virgin

his hand slipped
close to crotch
imagining machetes
sharp
and shiny in the sun

Colonizing Blackness

"We are all niggers!"   —Jim Jones

parroting Che,
he harnessed need,
bridled momentum,
and saddled history's haunches
to plow a new kingdom—
nigger hands
in nigger lands:
we are all niggers now

3.   A reoccurring perception, much like déjà vu, created when two disparate entities bear disquieting and instructive commonalities.

James Warren Jones ~~ May 13, 1931–November 18, 1978
Elvis Aaron Presley ~~ January 8, 1935 – August 16, 1977

Aping Orpheus

"enchanting his followers with his voice like Orpheus" — Protagoras

Tupelo is not,
after all, so far
away from Crete,
Indiana.

The same tracks
trail north and south
determining sides—
out and in, right and wrong,
black and white—
with gates ventricular and
labyrinthine.

Isolated
as each other's lost twin,
both carved a self
with ventriloquistvoice:
      aping Orpheus in a tongue stolen
      and enslaved.

Adamas

Suckling dissipation
and dregs
filtered through admonitions
not to be like Daddy,
they skimmed
shiny selves from sludge—
forging flesh from Mama's
molten shame, grown
luminous and faceted
with hope.

One little, two little . . .

The claim of Indian
blood made the swivel
more sure,
rooted the thick black hair
in mystery, remaking
history into a vast expanse
of warrior nobility and loss,
possible pasts
coloring the common truth
of little white boys
with dirty feet
eating peanut butter
and jelly on crooked
back steps.

1956

After years of wanderings
through mazes of back streets
ferreting pentecostal gospel,
the troubadour and the preacher
tapped the source:
                    Blackness,
a mother load
electric and Voltaic
as oil or coal,
a generator to amplify
their trumpetvoices
to all who would listen.

Joshuas both—
unshutting Jericho—
crooning down doors
and rolling the rocks
away.

The Nine Lives of Fidelity

There is another side to the good boys
who stand in the presence of women
out of deference to mama and wife.

Such chivalry only silver plates
their lust. The matted fur remains
hidden, hot and sticky underneath.

Unaccountable
for the partaking of fruits
forbidden, they stalk
certain they will not fall,
their landings always silent
as the padding paws
of cats.

virgula divina

"Some Sorcerers do boast they have a Rod . . ."   —Samuel Sheppard

When performance shifted from vertical to prone,
the two confused press with pleasure, heard

the cries of women unable to breathe as praise,
never learning to saddle desire with restraint:

> to poise weight upon elbows and knees—
> aloft and keen for divining.

The Wives

Their women, looking
so like Mama,
were pure ivory—
fair,
with fruitful virgin wombs—
pieta carved breast-smooth.

Sitting quiet as pretty
car ornaments, they grew
paler still,
exposed as they were
                in dashboard sun.

The Kings' New Clothes

Sometimes
screams tsunamied like love
but mostly came in waves
too insubstantial to plash
the unbearable wane of low tides
whose foamy recede was a revelation
exposing translucent flesh,
dewy,
horizon-flat,
and unbuoyant.

Which white
suit would cover the muck,
tide Mama's pride,
and cover the naked beaching
of these kings?

The King Is Dead: August 16, 1977

News spread like artificial
lights chasing the sunset.
People were surprised,
or sad, or indifferent,
and one,
sweltering by a ham radio,
stared straight into a tropic sun
filtered only by the synthetic
night of his shades,
saw the portent,
and wept.

4.   An entity, situation, memory, or place that eludes definition or fixedness.

Life in Jonestown was accompanied by the live or recorded voice of Jim Jones, which was broadcast throughout the community on loudspeakers nearly all of the time. Periodically, Jim Jones would gather the residents of Jonestown for what he called a White Night. During these hours long sessions he would preach to the congregants and then engage in suicide drills. The residents never knew whether a drill was real or "practice." There was a musical group in Jonestown called the Jonestown Express. Many children, who remain unaccounted, were born in Jonestown. Several people who lived in Jonestown, but survived, recalled the pervasive sound of the laughter of the youngest children.

White Night: Haiku

shrill as sudden night-
time sun was the scrutiny
of his always voice

"We got a hell of a lot of odds tonight. Anybody wants to leave now, before you—because this could be your night of death. Anybody want to leave? I'll let you go, because I know one thing, you'll never get in—they'll make your life more miserable when you get in the United States. I'll let your ass go. We'll help you through, so you won't get through the snakes and the—and the tigers. And the little frogs. You just touch, you die in a matter of minutes, if they touch you, happen to hop on you. Let's get down to the gut root, huh? I'm watc . . ."

There, there was music

They left many things
back home, but their sounds
rocked to sleep, stowaways
in knot-holed trunks. Blinded
by the unrelenting light at journey's
end, the displaced instruments
felt familiar fingers, heat-swollen
as forestfruit, and laughed.

At dusk, electric gospel, soul,
funk, and blues inflated
the rubbery nights with measured
breath that rippled across skin
like the sometime breeze
from the sea.

White Night X: Haiku

Evidence of true
conviction and loyalty
demanded forfeit.

"Not suicide. Suicide's an immoral act. He didn't–I wanted to clarify. Su–suicide is immoral, it's a way to get you back, coming right back through the thing. Only revolutionary suicide is justified, when you consider that this is a–there's no way to make any moral sense out of–of uh, further fighting, because it'd be maybe black people having to kill black people that they'd use to come after us and we would lose our moral impact, and thus make a witness like other communists have made, and uh, the great leader of the revolution here made, first revolt of the slaves, fifty years before USA, or many, many more–a hundred years before that here. Uh, do like Cuffy did, commit suicide. That's a revolutionary act. Rather than be taken prisoner, or go back into slavery."

There, there were flowers

Missing roses, she sought
a substitute. Fertilizer
was precious as the gold
lying buried in cheeks
of the distant sister rivers
snaking those soils.

Wakened by howling monkey
serenades, she disturbed
unnoticed the chickens
and pigs,
scraping from cages
the assurance of bloom.

There, there was loving

Another there found it strange,
the way the land began to curve:
the crescent path, so like his lover's hips
and farther, in the shadow of the fence—
the umbra outlines of her lips.

In time, she cocooned a half-moon
fetal enough to urge the flat
brown plateau middling her flesh
to swell to tortoiseshell.

White Night XII: Haiku

rain corrugated
and jagged fell metallic
and night blanched pale

"It ain't pleasant. I know it's not pleasant, children. But my God, somebody's gotta fight this revolution. I didn't ask for any considerations. I was young, just like you, and I chose to—when I coulda gone the easy way. If there is any easy way. A millionaire, and gave it up. Looks to me like you kids try to stay awake and carry this revolution, 'cause I'm long long in the battle. It's hell to plan this whole place, plan escape routes, plan—plan escape routes, plan how—if we go to the Soviet Union, plan if we all commit revolutionary suicide. Review it, because people's minds change. I don't like to do this . . ."

There, there was color

Having seen only flat toucans
named Sam on red cereal boxes,
the spectral angles of breathing birds,
cocky with fresh paint,
were a revelation reflected daily
in their American irises, green and blue,
and seventy shades of brown—
color surrounding pupils
vulnerable and open
at the center.

White Night XXI: Haiku

each test required
hands to relinquish palm press,
orphaning mercy

"Okay. You got revolutionary suicide and a task force that goes out to get our enemies. Take a potion and we go, all of us go. Or we go into the jungle. Or we make some kind of a militant stand here, demanding exodus. Oh, you can say, oh, we've been though that. Yeah, have we. I doubt if some people ever went through it. They just sit here. And maybe after the third and fourth time, it does go–it comes through their mind. Now I gave you some options. Which of those options do you vote for, and what is your position about oth–other everything? Go ahead, dear. . ."

There, there was laughter

Even the mosquitoes
didn't bother them—
small ones whose nascent gaze
cleared untamed horizon
with sheer infant determination
to secure the desired:
toy, bottle, snack, blanket, light, song,
shoulders—their laughter,
mosquito netting, fine and falling.

5.   A long-standing injustice, the injury of which is suffered as a direct result of another's duplicity.

In December of 1977, Lynetta Putnam Jones, Jim Jones's mother, died in Jonestown. She had joined her son and the members of the Peoples Temple in Jonestown only a few months before her death. Marceline Jones was Jim Jones's wife. She also resided in Jonestown. Marceline and Jones had a complex relationship. Before the massacre, she had written a note to him expressing her concerns for the safety of the children of Jonestown. She was able to save two of her own children by sending them to Georgetown during Congressman Leo Ryan's visit to Jonestown. Ryan was assassinated during his visit and remains the only congressman to die in the line of duty in the history of the United States. Christine Miller was a San Francisco Peoples Temple member who had moved to Jonestown. She challenged Jones when he began the ritual that led to the mass deaths. Drinking Flavor-Aid mixed with cyanide is thought to be the cause of death for many Jonestown residents. Of the more than 900 people who died at Jonestown, nearly 280 of them were under the age of 18.

Doubts

Warnings appear six-legged,
the occasional scurry
teasing the corner of the eye,
arm hairs soothed
by carefully averted gaze.

Distracted humming, a child's
talisman
against night noises.

No need to search for poison sprays
or imagine
what may lurk in crawling spaces.

Marceline Jones

Astride the laughter
of children playing nearby,
she paused for a moment
to look up,
her gaze shadowed by a hand
thinned to translucence—

finding no sign in the unrelenting
blue,
she moved on.

In the Marrow of the High Beam:
November 18, 1978

inside the skull walls
that pave the gray
matter of such times,
-the-painted-yellow-dashes-
down the middle
are sandbags
filled only with feathers

the dreadful coming
is a semi
whose tire rumble
laughs
at the audacity
of the broken line

tomorrow fading
into a futile fluttering
in the marrow of the high beam

Christine Miller

*"I feel like as long as there's life, there's hope. That's my faith"**

Like armor, her iron
words, alloyed and unrusted,
gallop in full grace.

*Jonestown resident, Christine Miller, in response to Jim Jones's final call for the community to commit mass suicide."

Inoculation

The only other times these two
tolerated a needle's pierce
so proximate to this unbroken,
beloved
infant flesh
was also for protection.

They believed the vial,
full of dark purple poison
injected into the soft space
of their son's toothless
and oblivious smile,
would provide sanctuary,
immunization
against invaders they could not see
but whose advance they heard,
artificially amplified,
as if
through a loudspeaker.

Hide and Seek

Hyacinth Thrush, 76 years old in 1978 and the one person found alive in the Jonestown compound, survived the mass deaths of her compatriots by hiding under her bed.

What lost or forgotten urge,
seven decades old,
led her first to knees—
to the familiar stance
of childhood prayers whispered
into the safe spaces
between her palms
and under her bed?

Hiding in the hollow caves
of those hours,
recalling the game
at which she had been
so good as a girl—
memory shifted her shape
small,
seeking sanctuary from
the "you're it"
staccatoed in shots, screams,
and the panting silence
of a night human
with sweat.

One

Under the pile,
as the stacked bodies
came to be called,
they found
one,
not poisoned
not shot,
but suffocated
under the deadweight
of her mother
and father.

Twenty-five pounds
pressed facedown
into the earth
with the urgent desire
of a farmer
who knows that the village
crop will not survive
under cloudless skies
but plants his seeds
nonetheless.

Bitter Almonds: A Found Poem

SUICIDE: THE
highly toxic chemical asphyxiant *ACT* that
interferes with
mur·der Pronunciation: \mər-dər\ Function: *noun*
the body's ability to use
oxygen. Exposure to sodium cyanide can be rapidly fatal. It
has whole-body (systemic) effects, particularly affecting
those organ systems most sensitive
Etymology: partly from Middle English *murther,*
from Old English *morthor;* partly from Middle English
murdre, from Anglo-French, of Germanic origin;
to low oxygen levels: the central nervous system
(brain), the cardiovascular system (heart and blood
vessels), and the pulmonary system (lungs). Sodium cyanide
is used commercially for fumigation, electroplating,
extracting *OF* **gold**
1: the crime of unlawfully killing a person especially with
malice aforethought   and *TAKING* **silver from ores, and**
chemical manufacturing. Hydrogen cyanide gas
released by sodium cyanide has a distinctive bitter
almond odor (others describe a musty "old sneakers
smell") but a large proportion of people cannot
INTENTIONALLY   **detect it; the odor does not**
provide adequate warning of hazardous concentrations. 2:
something very difficult or dangerous <the traffic was
murder> b: something outrageous or blameworthy <getting
away with murder>
Sodium cyanide is odorless when dry.
Sodium cyanide is shipped as pellets or briquettes. It
absorbs
ONE'S OWN

LIFE

Plain text: *Merriam Webster Dictionary*, "murder."
Bold text: Centers for Disease Control, "Cyanide poisoning."
Italicized, capitalized text: *Encyclopedia Britannica,* "suicide."

Schemata: A Requiem

XXXXX   XXXXXXX xxXXxxX XxxxX xXxXXXXXXx
xXxxxXxXXX XxxxX   XxxXXXXXxx XXxXXXX
XXXXxxXXXxXxXXX   XXXXxXXxXXXXxx
xXxXXX   XXXXXXXxxXxxXX
      XX   XXXxXxXXXXXXXxx XXXXX
      XXXXXXXxXxXXXXXXXx XxxX   XXXx
XXX   xXXX xXXXXX
      xXxxXXXXXXXX xXxXXX   XXXXXXXXXXxXxXX
XXXX   XXXxxXXXXX X XXXxxxXXXXX
XXXxX   XxXxxxXX XXXX   XXXXXX   XXX
xxxXXXXXXXX

  XXXXX XxxXxXXXXXXX   XXXXXxXXXXX XXXX
XxX XXXXX xxxXXX xXXxxXXXxXx XxXXXXX
XxxXxXXXX XXXXXXXXXXXxxxxX XXXXX
XXXX XXXX XXXxXXxxXXX   XXXXXxX XX XXx
                xXxxXXXX XXXXXXxxX
          xxXXxXXXXXXX Xx X XXXxXxXX XXX
XXX xxxx   XXXXXX xx XX XXX   XXXXX Xxx xXxx
XXXXXx XXX   XXXX XXX xxXx XXX x   X
xxxX xxxxxx
XXXXXXXXX   XXxXXXXXX   xxXX XXxxX
XX XXXXXXXXxx XXXXXXXXXxXX XXXXXXxxxX
xxXxxXxxxxXXXXXXXxx   xxx
      xxXXxxXXX xXX   XXXxxXXxx XXXX   XXxXx
XXXxxxXxXx XXXXXxXXx
  XXXXXX   XXXXX XXXXXXXXX xXxXX XXX xXx
XXXX xXX xXXXXXx   XXXXXXXxx
XxxXXXXxxXXXxx   XXXxXXXXxX XxXXxXX
XXx   XX   xx XXXXXXXX XXXXXXXXXXXx
xXXXXXXXxxX   XXXxXXXXXX   XXXXXXX
XxxXXX XXXxxxXx XXX XXXxxxxx XXXXXXX XXX
XXXxxx XXxxx Xxxx xxxX XX XXXXXXX   XXX
xxXXX   XXXXXXXXx xxxXX   XXX
   XXXXXXXXX   XXXXxx XxxXXXxxXxx
      XXxxxxX x xx XXXX xxx   XXXX

"More Than 900 Found Dead at Religious
     Compound in Guyana."
     Byline: November 25, 1978

No wail echoed the fall
of this scattered set of forms
lying earthen and unrequited,
face down in silent sleeping
as if
in defiance of some
never-to-come
kiss.

Alluvium

Recollection veins in rivulets,
its trace malleable,
fleeting as a flood plain—
an impressed hand upon the land,
with tawny tips dipped
and dissolving
in the sea.

The Children

What balm for loss so
green? Tossed overboard—bosky
dross—floating nameless.

6.   A profound, yet unfulfilled, desire or need.

When no one would claim his body, Jim Jones was unceremoniously buried at sea. There were approximately thirty-three residents of Jonestown who, for various reasons, survived November 18, 1978.

Lost at Sea

". . . they asked, "What have you done?'"   —*Book of Jonah 1:10*

This was no Jonah
cast out.

No intervening fish
will swallow this sinner

or womb his redemption
& resurrection.

Fathom

They found no record of the nights—
no letter,
note,
or tape
sounding the depth
of the obsidian nights
there in that place,
impenetrable
as the very beginning,
devoid of light
and the word.

Remains: Jonestown 2008

There is no assurance here,
blessed or otherwise,

no light
bright enough
to penetrate what remains—
to clean-scour
this vacant and vigorous
blossoming.

Vestigial Life

The stern-faced sepulcher furrows
its grim shutters
to protect the shrouded confessional,
abode for knees
the exact shade of plums.

Perhaps the knobby kneel
is complete, the throbbing
dying down at last
to indistinct and distant
thrumming.

The supplicant rises
from stones
worn rusty and concave
from the weight of years.

The bloodrush
needles the flesh,
threaded reddish-purple
and sharp.

There

On days without rain,
clouds, speeding to the sea, cast
caressing shadows.

About the Author

Carmen R. Gillespie received her Ph.D. from Emory University. She is professor of English and director of the Griot Institute for Africana Studies at Bucknell University in Lewisburg, Pennsylvania. She is a scholar of American, African American, and Caribbean literatures and cultures and a poet. In addition to journal and poem publications, she is the author of the books, *A Critical Companion to Toni Morrison* (2007), and *A Critical Companion to Alice Walker* (2011), and the editor of *The Clearing: Forty Years with Toni Morrison, 1970 - 2010* (2011). Carmen also has published a poetry chapbook, *Lining the Rails* (2008). She was the recipient of a 2005 Ohio Arts Council Individual Artist Fellowship for Excellence in Poetry. A Cave Canem Fellow and a Fulbright scholar, she has received awards and grants from the National Endowment for the Humanities, the Mellon Foundation, the Bread Loaf Writer's Conference, and the Fine Arts Work Center in Provincetown. In 2010, *Essence* magazine named Carmen one of its forty favorite poets in commemoration of the magazine's 40th anniversary. She shares her life with her husband, Harold Bakst, and daughters Chelsea and Delaney.